T

CW00327786

BY
Tom Stockdale

‖‖ •PARRAGON• ‖‖

This edition first published by
Parragon Book Service Ltd in 1996

Parragon Book Service Ltd
Unit 13–17 Avonbridge Trading Estate
Atlantic Road, Avonmouth
Bristol BS11 9QD

Produced by Magpie Books,
an imprint of Robinson Publishing

Illustrations courtesy of: Hulton Deutsch Collection;
Mirror Syndication International; Retna Pictures Limited

ISBN 0 75251 614 0

A copy of the British Library Cataloguing in Publication
Data is available from the British Library.

Typeset by Whitelaw & Palmer Ltd, Glasgow
Printed in Singapore

A DISTURBED
CHILDHOOD

Before Alberta and Marvin Pentz Gay Snr married in July 1935, Alberta had found it difficult to decide which of the two men courting her offered the best prospect of a secure family life. Gay's rival, Simon Rawlings was, like him, a Pentecostal preacher. Their faith was strong, and the House of God, as their church was called, observed strict Sabbath rules, fast days and female dress code. Its services were full of joyful gospel singing, and the spirit often took worshippers into a trance. Gay seemed the more charismatic of the two men, and it was not until after the marriage that Alberta learned of the violence within his family, a violence which would be carried over into the life of her eldest son.

They settled in a poor area of south-west Washington DC, and soon fell into disagreement over Alberta's infant son from a previous relationship. Gay sent young Michael to live with his aunt, wanting only his own offspring in the house. Their first child, Jeanne, was born two years later, but it was another two years before Gay had the son he claimed he really wanted. Born on 2 April 1939, Marvin Pentz Gay Jnr (Pentz was the name of the doctor who had delivered Gay Snr) would be loved by millions around the world, but would never find the love he hoped for from his father.

Growing up in a poor urban district during the 1940s was hard for any child, but the strict religious upbringing of the Gays made life even harder. Dancing, movies and television were banned, and the Sabbath marked a weekly isolation from the outside world. Still, this isolation also made the children feel special. By 1946, the six-year-old Marvin had two more siblings: Frankie, aged three, and Zeola ('Sweetsie'), still just a baby. And with the arrival of Alberta's cousin and her son, the household was a full one. But it was also a fearful one. Gay Snr ruled with a bible in one hand and a leather belt in the other, and none of the children were free from welts and bruises. Marvin Jnr was given especially harsh treatment. There was an instinctive antipathy between father and son and Gay Snr used to deny that Marvin was his child. Marvin later described the continual beatings which continued into his teenage years. 'By the time I was twelve', he said, 'there wasn't an inch of my body that hadn't been bruised and beaten by him.' Gay Snr would use psychological, as well as physical punishment, forcing the children to wait hours for a beating which they knew was coming.

Marvin's strong personality was evident from an early age, and it was soon obvious that he was determined not to give in to his 'peculiar, changeable, cruel and all-powerful king' of a father. The psychological pattern was set: Marvin used to goad his father into violence, as the only way he knew to attract his attention. This was a classic display of a child desperately hoping for a sign of love from an unloving parent, and drew Marvin closer to his mother.

One positive aspect of Marvin's relationship with his preacher father was accompanying him to his services. The whole family had good singing voices, but it was clear that Marvin had something special from when he was as young as three. The congregation began to expect the youngster to sing at their services, and Marvin loved their positive reaction. Throughout his life he was aware of the spiritual side of his voice as well as the artistic one, and fought a personal battle against the guilty feeling that his voice should be used for the glory of God rather than for the razzle-dazzle of the dance-floor.

At school, Marvin was a good-looking, studious and well-behaved pupil. His natural shyness and his father's profession made him a target for bullies, but he would always prefer running to fighting, and his natural athleticism made him a fast runner. Gay Snr also had an effeminate quality that made for easy insult, and Alberta Gay later commented that her husband liked to wear some items of her clothing. It was a predilection which inspired both fear and excitement in Marvin. On top of all this, Marvin's 'girlish' musical ability was another excuse to tease him. As well as singing constantly with schoolfriends, he had taught himself the piano, and he added drums and guitar to his repertoire during high school. Marvin's sporting prowess was a useful counter against the bullies, and he found boxing a particularly good way to attract the girls, as well as add prestige among his peers. If he hadn't decided to plump for music, Marvin later said he would have tried to become a professional sportsman.

Music, however, was always to the fore. Despite the mocking of other boys, singing in a group was another good way for a shy, handsome boy to get noticed by the girls, and Marvin's growing interest in the sounds of James Brown and Jackie Wilson led to his forming and playing piano for the DC Tones while at high school. Although he knew he had a good singing voice, Marvin was aware of its lack of power compared to the singers whose tones he loved. Feelings of inadequacy would plague him throughout his attempts to perfect a style he felt did not come naturally to him.

The DC Tones were short-lived, but the rise of doo-wop, with bands such as the Orioles and the Cadillacs, and the flurry of local doo-wop groups with their tight harmonies and gospel roots, thrilled the 16-year-old Marvin.

He hung around with a local group, the Rainbows, though he did not perform with them. He admired the skill of Clyde McPhatter and Ray Charles, and was struck by the style and the phrasing of Frank Sinatra, an artist whose mark would leave a lasting impression. Another influence was Billie Holiday, who reinforced Marvin's desire to use jazz in his own music, and although his own success would not come from jazz, the inheritance of Holiday's life-scarred voice would become especially poignant for the Marvin Gaye of the future.

Back at home, Alberta Gay was keeping the family alive through her work as a cleaner, while Gay Snr had a series of short-lived jobs bridging long periods of inactivity. Within his church – the House of God – disagreements and jealousies caused him to reduce his involvement, and by the end of the 1950s he had stopped any public religious activity, turning instead to the bottle. He became more than ever a problem within the family, embittered by his isolation from his 'calling', and making his relationship with Marvin even more strained.

By the age of 17 Marvin had decided upon a musical career, and he dropped out of high school. His father ordered him either to get a job or to join the Armed Services, so he took what he considered to be the more glamorous option and joined the Air Force. For the next year he was to regret his decision. He detested the military regime, and the nearest he got to flying was loading planes with fuel. Showing the contrariness of character that would become legendary, he began a deliberate policy of disobedience, only complying with orders if he felt like it. By the time Marvin was given an honourable discharge in less than a year later, he was considered to be crazy. He had gained more singing experience at Air Force dances, and lost his virginity to a prostitute – an important event for him.

His return home inevitably renewed the tension between Marvin and his father, and Marvin spent most of his time staying with friends. He soon joined a band with the remaining members of the Rainbows and, calling themselves the Marquees, they played around Washington until they met Bo Diddley, local black hero and R&B influence. Marvin would always acknowledge the effect that Diddley's strength and sensuality had on him.

With their new mentor, the Marquees set

about making an inroad on the touring circuit, and they cut a single in New York. 'Wyatt Earp/Hey, Little School Girl' never made the charts, but it helped Marvin to realise that he wanted to be the frontman, not an anonymous member of a harmony quartet. Maybe he remembered his feelings of triumph as a three-year-old Gospel singer. He began his first attempts at songwriting, but he still had much to learn.

Despite meeting Diddley, the group was forced to take menial jobs to make ends meet. It was especially galling for Marvin, because he knew that his father was willing him to fail.

The band's next step forward came with an introduction to Harvey Fuqua, who was the writer and lead singer with the Moonglows, a popular, though now flagging, doo-wop group with several R&B and pop hits and a successful association with Alan Freed, the man behind the rise of rock 'n' roll. Hearing the Marquees' version of the Moonglows' 'Ten Commandments Of Love', Fuqua invited them to join him as the new Moonglows, and in 1959 Marvin moved with the group to Chicago. Fuqua moulded them into a professional band, taught them technical skills and became a father figure to Marvin, who admired his world of 'cool times and hot women'.

Although they cut some records on the Chess record label (Marvin sang the lead on 'Mama Loochie') and sang backing vocals for artists such as Chuck Berry and Etta James, the Moonglows were forced to continue on the arduous touring circuit to survive, and had many unhappy experiences as a black group trekking around the Southern States in the late 1950s.

Life on the road was a natural place to learn about drugs and women. Although marijuana was all they could afford, Marvin's experimentations with drugs began at this time. His attractiveness to women helped him to overcome his shyness, and he had a relationship, sometimes a violent one, with a dancer in the tour party. Despite the harsh conditions and a strict taskmaster in Fuqua, Marvin's confidence grew. Although he did not fully realize it, his looks and his voice were turning into a knockout combination. Fuqua recognized this, and Marvin needed no persuasion to break up the band and move to Detroit, where the perceptive Fuqua had decided that the next musical movement was going to break. It was 1960, and his timing was spot on.

THE SOUND OF
YOUNG AMERICA

Harvey Fuqua's music business contacts already included a Detroit record label called Anna, run by Gwen and Anna Gordy, and he and Marvin signed to the label, though they would not actually record for it. Fuqua formed two small companies, Harvey and Tri-Phi, and Marvin did drumming and piano session work for its artists. Fuqua's relationship with Gwen Gordy became a romantic one, and they married in 1960, while Marvin turned his attention to Anna Gordy. The sisters were an admired force on the Detroit music scene, and Marvin's pursuit of a woman 17 years his senior was seen as a career move as much as a love match. Outsiders, however, did not know of the influence of Marvin's mother, and the attraction of an older woman was as understandable as his need for a father figure to make up for the poor relationship he had with his natural father. Marvin was an astute as well as a thoughtful man, aware of what people might be thinking about his relationship with Anna, and although the attraction was based on love, he agreed that 'Marrying a queen might not make me a king, but at least I'd have a shot at being a prince'.

His career took a more promising turn when Harvey, Tri-Phi and the Gordy sisters merged with the record company that was starting to make waves around Detroit. It was run by the girls' brother, Berry Gordy, and its name was just changing from Tamla to Tamla Motown.

Berry Gordy was an ambitious music lover whose jazz record shop had closed in 1955. Gordy was forced to work on the Ford car production line, but began composing songs which soon got him noticed. He attracted the attention of Jackie Wilson with 'Reet Petite' and Barrett Strong, with 'Money (That's What I Want)', and by 1958 he had left the car industry and gathered several hopeful, talented songwriters and producers together. His gift for spotting popular musical potential was proved when he picked up the rejected Matadors and started to work with their singer, William 'Smokey' Robinson.

The Tamla label, opened soon afterwards, relied on major record companies for distribution, and Tamla saw little of the profit from any success it had until Gordy organized national distribution. Almost the whole of the Gordy family was gathered into the new business, and a house was bought as a headquarters. The sign hanging outside it gave a correct indication of the company's potential, 'Hitsville USA'.

Berry Gordy wanted the black music which was being successfully copied by white artists, to be sung by – and controlled by – the people who wrote it. At that time it was not fashionable for white pop fans to have black artists in their record collections. Gordy's overall game plan was to attract the massive white audience to the black sounds which were almost always contained within their own chart, the R&B chart.

The young singer, 1963

Gordy rapidly built a company full of talented people who were willing to work extremely long hours for little financial reward (three dollars a week on average), but they worked, at least at first, in a family atmosphere. Given the alternative of work in a car plant, the possibility of greater gain was good enough for all of them, Marvin Gay included. He joined a growing team of artists who were merely the icing on the rich cake of writers and producers, and who soon honed a studio sound which everybody now knows as the Motown Sound. Gordy's corporate slogan described Motown as 'the sound of young America', but he also dissected it into 'rats, roaches, talent, guts and love'.

Marvin's session work was spread around the whole Motown roster: his drumming with the Marvelettes helped to give the company their first crossover number one on the white-dominated pop charts with 'Please Mr Postman' in 1961, which beat James Darren and Chubby Checker to the top. During the same year, Motown signed the groups which would become the Supremes, the Pirates and the Temptations. Marvin worked hard and was liked by the staff at Motown – his politeness and sensitivity were remarked upon by the women – but he wanted to be more than a popular session musician. He wanted to be the black Frank Sinatra. Marvin saw himself as a crooner, and it would always be a disappointment to him that the music he made in that vein never sold as well as his soul music.

At Motown there was a conveyor-belt style of song production that gave whoever was making a dent in the charts, the first choice of

material, although it was also common
practice for several producers to be given the
same material to see who could make it the
greatest success. Marvin hadn't had any hits,
so he was scrambling around at the bottom
with the other young hopefuls, although he
did have the ear of Berry Gordy through
Anna, and Gordy was the man who decided
which records would be released. He rejected
hundreds of songs by artists who had already
proved their talent, but proof that his system
worked was the chart success that Motown
was already enjoying – and the flood that was
soon to follow.

Anna Gordy was good for Marvin. She
believed in his talent and helped him to
overcome his lack of confidence in his style of
singing. His songwriting was improving too.
Still, his first attempt at finding a place on the

Motown conveyor-belt was an album containing almost all covers. Marvin's first single was an original co-composition with Berry Gordy, 'Let Your Conscience Be Your Guide'. The credits on 'Let Your Conscience' showed Marvin's altered surname for the first time – from Gay to Gaye. This may have stopped the mocking Marvin had endured all his young life, but it did not help to sell the single, nor the album, *The Soulful Moods of Marvin Gaye*, from which it was taken. He didn't have the maturity to carry the classics he was attempting, and Motown was geared up for dancers, not lounge lizards. His next two singles were also failures, but Marvin was learning fast, and knew that he needed to follow the house style to be able to release any further songs.

He continued to work at his writing, and

hung around with Smokey Robinson and another new signing, the eleven-year-old 'Little' Stevie Wonder. His reward finally came with 'Stubborn Kind of Fellow', a song he co-wrote with producer Mickey Stevenson. It became an R&B hit and gave Marvin his place on the bus for the Motown Revue, a cramped, overworked, underpaid show alongside some of the greatest names of soul music: the Marvelettes, the Miracles, Mary Wells, 'Little' Stevie Wonder and the Supremes performed up to six shows a day, as well as providing each other with backing vocals. 'It was some of the hardest work I've ever done', Marvin reflected later. Compared to the other artists in the Revue, Marvin's stage show was understated. He refused to go through the Motown 'charm school' which had been teaching professional techniques to acts who, for the most part, came from the streets, and his natural lack of feeling for dance led to his static, finger-clicking style. He needn't have worried, as his charisma was worth more than any rehearsed routine.

Marvin's self-confessed inability to dance seems at odds with his next single, 'Hitch Hike', released in late 1962, which accompanied a popular dance step he claimed to have invented. 'Hitch Hike' was a successful crossover record, reaching number 30 on the pop chart. Its follow-up, 'Pride and Joy', confirmed Marvin's commercial status by reaching the top ten. Performing backing vocals on the single were Martha and the Vandellas, who later benefited from Marvin's authorship of 'Dancin' In The Streets'. 'Pride and Joy' was produced by the recently formed trio of Holland, Dozier and Holland, who would sprinkle their magic upon the whole of

Marvin, 1964

Motown. The album, *That Stubborn Kind of Fellow*, released in 1963, contained all Marvin's singles to date, as well as 'Wherever I Lay My Hat (That's My Home)', which would be a 1983 hit in Britain for Paul Young. With his marriage to Anna Gordy during 1963, it seemed as though Marvin Gaye had arrived. And his artistry was held firm by Anna's sound business sense: something which came to Marvin as naturally as dancing!

A HOT PROPERTY

Now aged 24, Marvin was able to move his parents into a better area of Washington, and from now on he would always send enough money to his mother to prevent her having to take cleaning jobs. He got on no better with his father, though; his role had been taken on by Berry Gordy, who, ten years Marvin's senior, was a model of strength and ambition. Gordy drove the company at a furious pace – artists were continually on the road or in the studio, but the results were starting to show, and he believed that the momentum must be maintained. Marvin had already shown the obstinacy of his character and although he and Gordy had several clashes during Marvin's career, at this time it was a positive relationship. Marvin's advancement was obvious on the 1963 album, *Marvin Gaye – Live On Stage*, and in the singles, 'Can I Get A Witness' (number 22 in the pop charts) and 'You're A Wonderful One' (number 15). He was amongst the front-runners in the Motown stable, and the Motown Revue programme of 1964 had him as top billing.

Berry Gordy's idea of pairing Marvin Gaye with a new signing, Mary Wells, paid off all round when Wells hit the big time with 'My Guy', before the duet album had even been released. The duet format became Marvin's home territory for a time, as his smooth image

The rising star

and boyish charm made him the perfect eligible young man for the black female record-buying public. The album, *Together*, was light on material, but it was an R&B number one, and the single from it, 'Once Upon A Time', gave Marvin his first chart success in Britain. 'How Sweet It Is (To Be Loved By You)', released towards the end of 1964, continued his solo success (reaching number 49 in Britain), although another attempt to crack the crooners' market, 'When I'm Alone I Cry', was a failed one.

In November 1964 Marvin flew to London, an event in itself as he had a fear of flying. It was partly Motown's declared riposte to the Beatles' 'invasion' of America earlier that year, and partly an attempt to push Marvin towards a British hit, to which end he appeared on the television pop show *Ready,*

Steady, Go! Motown had suddenly hit pay dirt with the Supremes, who reached number one in Britain during that month with 'Baby Love', and the American chart showed the growing influence of the black-owned company that autumn, with songs from the Supremes, the Four Tops and Martha and the Vandellas reaching the top 20. An amazing three-quarters of its 60 singles had charted in America.

With the meteoric rise of the Supremes – they notched up five successive number one singles – Berry Gordy's time was increasingly tied up with them, and especially with Diana Ross. Marvin felt keenly the absence of the man who, despite running a fast-growing company, had always had a lot of time for his young star. He had shown Gordy that he could carry a song into the charts, and he began to feel that

he deserved more artistic freedom. 1965 was
the year that the Temptations and the Four
Tops pushed Motown further into the spot-
light, but Marvin was busy in other directions.
He and Anna adopted a son. Marvin Pentz
Gaye III gave their marriage the boost it
needed: Marvin's endless touring and recording schedule had given them both the opportunity to have affairs, and cracks were
appearing in their relationship.

Marvin had already begun a habit of dropping
out of live engagements, blaming stage fright
for his behaviour. But he also believed that he
had done enough rigorous touring and he
fought against the Motown show business
packaging. During one gig, he came onstage
and to everyone's surprise sang mostly stan-
dards rather than the hits they were all waiting
for. His live shows of 1965 were sold out, but

his next album, *Hello Broadway*, consisted mainly of versions of songs from musicals, and gained much less attention than his two singles earlier in the year, 'I'll Be Doggone' and 'Ain't That Peculiar', both Smokey Robinson creations, and both reaching number 8 in the pop charts. Robinson praised Marvin for the ease with which his vocals lifted the songs, and Marvin reciprocated by acknowledging Smokey's talent at a time when his own writing was not going so well.

Marvin and Smokey both had a taste for recreation and started playing golf together. Marvin's new riches and love of sport also led him to help finance the Detroit Wheels, the city's football team, and to back the boxer Tommy Hanna. His other growing recreation was drug use. He had discovered a fondness for cocaine, believing the drug inspired him,

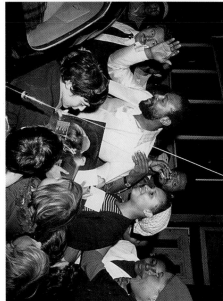

Young fans press in

and it would not be much longer before the recreation became a habit, and the habit a dependency.

Marvin wound up 1965 with another cabaret album, *A Tribute To The Great Nat King Cole*, who had died in February. Despite his feeling that Motown was not helping to market him in the way he wanted, he was allowed to make the records of his choice. But he was jealous of the amount of success that other Motown acts like the Supremes, the Miracles and Stevie Wonder were having. His frustration was also apparent in his home life. He and Anna were having public screaming matches, at odds with the public's image of the smooth and loving duettist. Marvin was given a new duet partner in 1966. Kim Weston's mellow voice was a soulful match with Marvin's, and their album *Take Two* showcased them both to good effect, and included the single 'It Should Have Been Me' and the hit 'It Takes Two'. Further collaboration was prevented by Weston's departure from Motown.

Despite more solo success with 'One More Heartache' and 'Take This Heart Of Mine', and an appearance on *The Ed Sullivan Show*, Marvin was still looking for his first number one record in 1967. Berry Gordy suggested another partner to lift his career and, as with so many things Gordy suggested, the idea worked. The 21-year-old Tammi Terrell, seven years younger than Marvin, was loved by everyone at Motown for her bubbly, gutsy personality and vocal talent. In the studio they were a perfect match, and the songs written for them by Motown's latest team of Ashford and Simpson made them sound like the lovers they never were. They were produced by Johnny

Bristol and Harvey Fuqua, who understood more than most people how to get the best performance from Marvin.

Once he was in the studio, Marvin was in his element. His vocal range allowed him to do all his own harmony work, and his arrangements had a freshness that stood out. However, he was relying more on cocaine than before, claiming that it gave him a clean feeling that he found nowhere else.

From their first single together, Marvin and Tammi showed that they had something special. 'Ain't No Mountain High Enough' was the start of a two-year, three-album collaboration, and reached number 19 in the pop charts. 'Your Precious Love' climbed to number 5 just after the release of the album *United*, which showed Marvin and Tammi's talents with a variety of styles. However, in the summer of 1967, Tammi collapsed on stage with what was later diagnosed as a brain tumour. She began a battle to recover her health, during which her good humour seldom wavered. Marvin was sent out to concerts with a replacement, Barbara Randolph, as he was in such demand as a duettist. As a result, his solo work did not sell so well.

Tammi Terrell came into the studio in a wheelchair to record their second album, *You're All I Need*, which was released halfway through 1968. It contained the number 8 hit single 'Ain't Nothing Like The Real Thing' and 'You're All I Need To Get By', which reached number 7 in the pop charts (number 19 in Britain). Marvin's solo work at this time included the singles 'You' and 'Chained'. His output was nothing if not prolific – the long working hours which had helped to spoil his marriage were now a refuge from a failed one. He was also deeply upset by Tammi's illness, and in one moment of despair he shut himself in his room with a gun and threatened to kill himself.

Many great works of art have been created out of depression, and so it was for Marvin. Producer Norman Whitfield got him in to the studio to record a song which Gladys Knight and the Pips had made a hit the year before – 'I Heard It Through The Grapevine'. Marvin's soaring version shot to the top in December 1968 and remained there for seven weeks, selling nearly four million copies. It would also reach number 1 in Britain, and a tour there was promised, but never materialized. Marvin regained his place among Motown's elite, although he said he was loathe to continue bringing out R&B-based records and wanted to move beyond the form.

The album containing 'Grapevine' was *In The Groove*, which, because of the single's success, helped to revitalize Marvin's solo career. Yet it was not until his next album, *MPG*, in May 1969, that Marvin cracked the top 50 with a long player – partly because Motown had a policy of releasing any material considered worthwhile as a single. The album – the name was Marvin's initials – was nicknamed 'Miles Per Gallon' in Britain, and, with the exception of 'Too Busy Thinking About My Baby', contained enough sad songs to make any sensitive listener wonder if anything was going well in Marvin's life. As a release from his endless recording schedule, he had been trying his hand at producing fellow Motown

Acclaim by the audience

artists, the Originals. He and they were rewarded with three hit singles.

The third Gaye/Terrell album was released towards the end of 1969. Entitled *Easy*, it contained the hit singles 'What You Gave Me' and 'The Onion Song'. Years later, Marvin admitted that it was Valerie Simpson, of the Ashford and Simpson writing partnership, who had sung Tammi's vocal tracks on most of the album. Marvin had agreed to the plan because it would allow the ailing singer's family to collect royalties, and Simpson's voice bore a startling resemblance to Tammi's. Terrell's illness beat her in early 1970, and Marvin, who had watched her fight and lose, was grief stricken, and vowed never to do a duet again.

WHAT'S GOING ON

The beginning of the new decade was a time of change for Motown. It had lost Holland, Dozier and Holland in arguments over royalties, and Diana Ross had sung her last song with the Supremes, before beginning the solo career for which Berry Gordy had been grooming her. In addition, Motown itself split with Detroit by moving to Los Angeles, leaving many of its team behind, and effectively ending the 'family' atmosphere.

Marvin was now 30, and spent plenty of time contemplating his situation, Tammi's death, the state of his marriage, the direction of his music. He adopted a more laid-back dress style and grew a beard. His first album of the new decade was *That's The Way Love Is* in January 1970. One of its few highlights was 'Abraham, Martin and John', a foretaste of the politically aware mood to come. After Tammi's death, however, Marvin was reluctant to visit the studio, and he didn't perform for a couple of years. There were rumours that he had retired which Motown, who didn't know what he was up to, tried to dispel with a couple of 'Greatest Hits' selections and an announcement that he was busy in the studio.

Marvin had remained in Detroit when the Motown move took place, and he took advantage of his sporting friendships to begin training with the Detroit Lions football squad. He convinced himself that he was good enough for the team, although it was clear that, whatever potential he had when younger, it was too late for him to start a professional sporting career. However, it took him out of seclusion, got him fit and started him thinking positively. At the same time, through his work with the Originals, he learned a lot about the technical side of running a studio, especially with regard to the over-dubbing of vocals for harmony parts.

Back in the world of music, the Jackson Five were making an instant success as Motown's new signing, with songs including 'I Want You Back', 'ABC' and 'I'll Be There'. Elsewhere, the background of the Vietnam War was making waves in the growing politicization of music, as was shown in 1970 by the huge success of Edwin Starr's 'War'. Marvin found a new interest in life by thinking about the troubles that were going on at home and abroad. The catalyst was the return of his brother Frankie from his term in Vietnam, and the stories Frankie told made Marvin's blood boil. In a pattern that would repeat itself in his best work from now on, Marvin's musical impetus now came from someone else. 'Obie' Benson of the Four Tops wrote the song 'What's Going On' with Al Cleveland, though there would be disputes over its authorship. Marvin made the song undeniably his own, and proceeded to collaborate with other writers on new material.

Marvin was unwittingly at the forefront of a major change in direction for the writing of

popular music, which had been greatly
influenced by the Beatles. The rise of the
singer/songwriter started the demise of the
writer/production teams, with which Motown
had created its 'sound' and its reputation. As
Marvin said, 'the artists' time had arrived'. For
Motown, it was Marvin and Stevie Wonder
who were to benefit most directly from the
new artistic freedom, but it did not happen
without a fight. In Marvin's case, Motown
were not at all keen to release the material that
he presented them with on the album *What's
Going On*, and it was only because he threatened never to record anything for them again
that release was allowed in May 1971. His faith
in himself was proved by public reaction; the
album reached number 6 in the American
charts and made Marvin a serious artist in the
eyes of the world. It brought his recently
honed vocal layering skills together with the

Marvin sings

spiritual content that he had grown up with in an argument for peace, which gave rise to the 'concept' album. It contained three top ten singles: 'What's Going On', 'Mercy Mercy Me' and 'Inner City Blues'. Smokey Robinson called it 'Marvin Gaye's masterpiece, the greatest album, in my opinion, ever made by anyone'.

Marvin at last had financial security, and had rediscovered the God he thought he had lost by making secular music. The only downside was that he failed to win the Grammy that he and many others had expected for the album; Carole King's *Tapestry* won best album and Lou Rawls took the best R&B Male Vocal award.

For a while, Marvin simply enjoyed the wave of success that *What's Going On* brought. He was in demand for public appearances; he agreed to some, but broke all but one of them, feeling that he had given the world a classic album and that he deserved a break from that part of his professional life. The one event he turned up for was in Washington on 1 May 1972. The nervous organisers enlisted the help of Marvin's mother to make sure he turned up, and the tactic worked. The town declared it 'Marvin Gaye Day' and he was presented with the keys to the city after an address at his old school, where he warned students of the dangers of drug-taking. The evening's concert was a triumph; the *Washington Post*'s review described him as 'a man responsible for radically changing the style of soul music', and he sang 'What's Going On' four times that day.

He continued the habit of breaking engagements, but managed a concentrated period of work in a new direction. The success of Isaac Hayes' soundtrack for the film *Shaft* led Marvin to write the soundtrack for *Trouble Man*. The plot read like a black urban version of a spaghetti western, and the movie itself was a failure. Marvin's soundtrack, released in December 1972, gave him the chance to write in the jazz-coloured style that Motown could not sell. The album was one of only two for which he wrote every track unaided, and it sold well. The album cover, with prophetic coincidence, featured his name and the title surrounded by bullet holes.

Marvin also took up two acting offers at the time; back in 1964 he had been offered the lead role in a biopic of the recently deceased Sam Cooke, but the manner of Cooke's death – he was shot - made Marvin too nervous to consider it. Neither *The Ballad of Andy Crocker* or *Chrome and Hot Leather* gained enough acclaim for him to continue with acting, though he allocated some of the blame to Motown and Berry Gordy, who were putting a lot of time and money into Diana Ross's move into movies.

Even so, he agreed to record an album with Ross, thus breaking his promise never to sing duets again. It was a reversion to the traditional Motown style of recording, but the songs were not really strong enough to pass the test of time. Of course, when it was released, late in 1973, the presence of the two top vocalists was bound to make the album sell, and a clutch of singles went into the top twenty, even though it lacked the intimacy of Marvin's work with Tammi Terrell. The promotional campaign for the record tried to emphasise the harmony between the stars, although the truth was that Marvin's use of marijuana in the studio upset the pregnant Ross, and many of the vocal tracks were recorded separately.

By now Marvin had followed Motown to Los Angeles, where he also bought a house for his parents. Though he fought every step of the way for musical independence, he never tried to break away from his reliance on his mother for security. His image of the perfect woman combined notions of security and maternity with the sexual traits of prostitutes, whom he visited to satisfy his need for 'no strings' relationships. His public image as a sex-symbol gave him ample opportunity to experience the sexual world, but he was always looking for his perfect woman; in 1973 Marvin believed he had found her.

LOVE AND LOATHING

Marvin was working on the official follow-up to *What's Going On*, when he was introduced to 16-year-old Janis Hunter, who had come to the studio with her mother to meet Marvin through his writing partner, Ed Townsend. He was immediately struck by her, and his music was given an emotional boost by his passion for a girl who was not only a minor, but 17 years younger than him. The album was *Let's Get It On*, released in the autumn of 1973, and its theme was sex and love. The title track was a

Performance

number one single, selling more copies than 'I Heard It Through The Grapevine' and helping Marvin's current contract renegotiations. The album continued Marvin's singing of his beliefs with total honesty – it was direct communication between himself and his listener, and it reached number 2 in the charts, despite receiving some negative reviews. Songs like 'You Sure Love to Ball' brought accusations of offensiveness, but Marvin defended himself against such complaints, and many reviews backed him: one British reviewer called the album 'the most incredible collection of screwing music available'.

A profitable new contract and a hit album, plus the duets with Diana Ross, gave Marvin any number of choices about the direction he could now take. To many people's surprise, he took to the hills, renting a beautiful, secluded cabin with views which enraptured him. He also took Janis Hunter. She was his perfect woman, and he felt as though he was living in heaven, away from the prying eyes of the world, the pressures of business and the anger of his wife. He was supporting his parents as well as his family, and was becoming concerned about the amount of money Anna might claim if they divorced.

He surprised everyone by turning up for a performance at the Oakland Coliseum on 4 January 1974, which was released later that year as *Marvin Gaye Live*! He played up to his sex-star image, though at the beginning he had been so nervous about the possibility of the sell-out crowd not applauding him that he sent his brother Frankie on stage ahead of him. Frankie bore more than a passing resemblance to Marvin and so received a tumultuous welcome, which of course turned to confusion when Marvin himself came on stage a minute later. His wildly received set included a new song called 'Jan', which was not recorded for any studio album. He was, however, keeping Janis herself hidden from the outside world.

He came out of his retreat in the summer of 1974 and moved to Hollywood, after his guard dogs were inexplicably killed. And in August he set off on a 20-date American tour, partly for the guaranteed box office receipts, and partly to silence those who were saying that he wouldn't be able to do it. His entourage included his mother (without whom he said he couldn't play live), a dance troupe and a 20-piece orchestra, and the tour was a sell-out. However, the strain took its toll, as much from the increased amount of drugs he took as from the nerves which he felt made drug use necessary.

He was desperate to get back to the pregnant Janis, who delivered a baby girl, named Nona, in September. Marvin immersed himself in his new family, and so began another period without a new release. In 1975, as Stevie Wonder collected Grammies ('like Disney collects Oscars', said Marvin) and Lionel Ritchie and the Commodores began to make their presence felt, Marvin received notice that Anna was beginning divorce proceedings against him.

He treated the situation in the same way that he treated his business and tax affairs, or anything else he didn't want to think about: he ignored it. He had always spent money

The lights and the glitter

like water – he had recently completed
building a recording studio on Sunset
Boulevard and he continued to finance
boxers. It was as though he thought that if he
spent the money, his wife or the taxman
would give him up as a lost cause. Janis soon
became pregnant again, and they moved to a
ranch in the San Fernando valley.

His moods were changeable, and although
Janis read them and accepted them, he started
to lose control of the relationship in
arguments, in the same way that his
relationship with Anna had begun to
deteriorate. He would later describe himself
as a man of two contradictory halves, who
allowed the darker side to gain dominance,
despite the attractions of showing the loving,
generous side. And he was prepared to
catalogue his feelings and fantasies in his

music, laying out for inspection a man struggling with himself.

The birth of a son, Frankie (nicknamed Bubby), in November 1975 gave the 36-year-old Marvin another period of familial calm. He had performed at a couple of benefit concerts, appearing at one of them with his head shaven as a protest against the imprisonment, for murder, of boxer Ruben Carter. But as far as a recording schedule was concerned, Marvin thought it was something for the artist to decide upon, not the record company, and he took no notice of any piece of paper which might say differently. However, he was persuaded back into the studio, when Berry Gordy played him some songs that writers Leon Ware and T-Boy Ross (Diana's brother) had composed. Marvin knew them from Motown's early days, and Ware came onboard as producer. Amidst large quantities of cocaine, breaks for basketball and regularly delayed starts, Ware witnessed his work being turned into, what could only be described as, Marvin's songs. The album, *I Want You*, was released in March 1976, and the songs were in the *Let's Get It On* mood, sexy and physical. It sold a million copies, and although Marvin was pleased, he admitted it was not a progression from his last album; it was simply something he had done because he was not doing anything else.

As 1976 continued, Marvin realised that he was running out of money. His extravagant lifestyle, his failed sporting and business ventures and his drug habit had made holes in his bank balance. He surrounded himself with people who, his friends agreed, were out to get what they could from him, and succeeded

Marvin Gaye, 1976

by indulging his weaknesses – drugs, women and parties. He decided to go on tour, which was the quickest way to earn some money and a way of avoiding a lawsuit for non-payment of alimony and child-support to Anna.

In September he flew to London for the first time in ten years at the start of a European tour. The English dates were topped by three nights at the London Palladium, where his sensual show was recorded for later release. His audiences were not slow in showing their appreciation and Marvin was surprised and gratified at such attention from a group of fans he had ignored for a decade.

Live! At the London Palladium was released in March 1977 and contained three sides which recalled a memorable evening. Side four had proved a problem due to the limited amount of material recorded, until Marvin's engineer, Art Stewart, presented him with a tape he had painstakingly worked on from a piece Marvin had been playing around with in the studio. Art used to record any little snippets for Marvin's future reference, and the 'doodle' in question became an almost 12-minute track called 'Got To Give It Up'. Although Marvin took very little notice of the disco fever that was topping the charts at the time, he liked some of its more funky incarnations and 'Got To Give It Up', a relaxed Marvin Gaye vocal track with an added dance rhythm, became a number 1 in America (number 7 in Britain), and Marvin started to use it to kick off his concerts.

In the same month that *Live! At The London Palladium* was released, Marvin's divorce from

Anna came through. The financial settlement was an imaginative coup from Marvin's lawyer, who was well aware that his client's finances could not meet the $1 million that Anna was demanding. He got both parties to agree that Anna would receive the $305,000 advance from Marvin's next album, plus another $295,000 of its royalties. Marvin was in no position to argue; he was being sued by several people, including his ex-manager and several musicians for unpaid salaries, and his taxes were in a mess.

He toyed with the idea of making a quick, worthless album to get the debt out of the way, and then decided to go to the other extreme. The result was *Here, My Dear,* a double album which chronicled the story of the marriage, ending with a number describing the new love he had found. 'I just sang and sang until I'd

Marvin Gaye

drained myself of everything I'd lived through,' he said. It took a year before he was happy with it, and he then asked Anna to come and listen to it. She did, and left without saying a word. She was later reported to be considering a lawsuit for invasion of privacy. 'All's fair in love and war' retorted Marvin. *Here, My Dear* was finally released in December 1978 and reached number 26 in the album charts.

By this time Marvin had been married to Janis for 14 months. It seemed an unfortunate match, as their co-habitation was not exactly successful. Marvin's jealousy showed itself in a paranoid form: he didn't want to lose Janis to anyone, but at the same time he tried to force her to have affairs, as though he wanted her to let him down. The pressure put on them both was intense, and Marvin returned to his 'selectively promiscuous' lifestyle.

The costs of the divorce added to Marvin's other financial obligations and disasters, including the closing down of his studio by the taxman, and he was forced to file for voluntary bankruptcy in mid-1978. From the court records, it seemed that he owed nearly everyone whom it was possible to owe. 'I prefer to handle my own life and affairs', he explained in an interview, but admitted, 'I'm not the smartest in business.'

Yet, in September, he was signing a lucrative seven-year contract with Motown, placing a deep-down loyalty to Berry Gordy before all of his complaints about poor treatment and renumeration. His life was series of ups and downs, seemingly running concurrently, and as 1979 approached nothing appeared to be changing.

Anguish

BACK IN THE HIGH LIFE

For his fortieth birthday Marvin had a party —
a joyful occasion attended by Berry Gordy,
Smokey Robinson and Stevie Wonder.
Although *Here, My Dear* had received poor
reviews, he was determined to shut up the
critics with a commercial follow-up. Motown
was full of new young faces, Bloodstone,
Teena Marie and Rick James. The British
punk explosion had sent record companies
scurrying around with blank cheques for
bands who'd scarcely learned their instru-

ments. Michael Jackson was becoming a one-man recording industry and an artist with the temerity to be called Prince, set Marvin's competitive teeth on edge.

Once again, with the need for cash dominant in his mind, Marvin took to the road. He set out in a well-equipped bus to escape the need for flying, but collapsed part-way through the tour from physical exhaustion coupled with drug over-use. In the meantime, Janis had taken the children with her to her mother's house, so Marvin's mother took him home to hers.

Three more blows during the year pushed Marvin right down into the pit. He recorded the new album, entitled *Love Man*, but it was rejected by Motown, who wanted it reworked before they would release it. Then

Andy Price, a boxer Marvin financed, had a shot at the welterweight title against Sugar Ray Leonard. A win would have restored Marvin's financial resources in one go, but Price didn't make it through the first round. And finally, Janis did run off with another man; and it wasn't just *any* other man, it was singer Teddy Pendergrass. What Marvin had most feared and most expected had finally happened, and he had no one to blame but himself.

Unable to face Los Angeles, Marvin went to Hawaii and Japan on tour, and then returned to Hawaii in late 1979, where he met up with Janis and the children. They ended up fighting, however, and Janis returned home again to her mother, though she left Bubby with Marvin. By April 1980, Marvin was living on a cliff in a converted bread van, penniless, and suffering from cocaine-derived impotence. Bubby was the only joy in the darkness of his mental breakdown.

Once again, in his despair he picked up his music again, and started reworking the *Love Man* tracks. He was persuaded to comply with an agreement to do a European tour which had already been postponed once, and flew to London in June with several friends and family members. The main advantage of a tour outside America was that the American tax department could not confiscate Marvin's foreign earnings to pay off some of the $2 million it claimed he owed.

The tour threw him back into the privileged and stressful world of 'Marvin Gaye – superstar'. Drugs and women thrust themselves at him, while the tour management

64

Montreux Festival, 1980

tried to keep him on a tight rein, which was understandable considering his reputation. Even so, he ducked out of a concert in Manchester by escaping through a toilet window, simply as a reaction against the schedule he was being forced to keep. His greatest show of obstinacy was on 8 July 1980, when he announced that he was not going to show up at a benefit in the presence of Princess Margaret, a fan of Marvin's music. By the time he was coaxed into performing, the Princess had left and a public insult to royalty had been achieved.

Despite the upsets in England, the prospect of returning to America, his tax problems and the threat of divorce from Janis made London seem a more attractive proposition, so Marvin stayed on after the tour. The party scene was good, and he took advantage of his female following, as well as continuing work on tracks old and new.

London suddenly became the place to be for Motown when it realised that Stevie Wonder's British tour coincided with a visit by Diana Ross, and with Marvin already there, it seemed a heaven-sent opportunity, especially in the year of the record company's belated 20th anniversary celebrations. Stevie managed to get Diana and Marvin to appear with him, and the crowd at his Wembley Arena concert of 7 September was treated to a ten-minute meeting of giants.

The Marvin Gaye album which Motown brought out in January 1981 was not a commercial successor to *I Want You*. Marvin claimed that the tapes had been smuggled back to America before they were finished;

Marvin Gaye

even the name of the album, *In Our Lifetime*, was wrong, for he had planned a question mark to come at the end. He had been reworking *Love Man*, combining its sexual lyrics with his recent feelings about nuclear apocalypse. So angry was he at Motown's action that he dissociated himself from the album and announced that he would never work with them again.

Marvin returned to depression, drugs and disorder, though he allowed interviewers to see the state in which he was living. He was rescued from this condition by Belgian promoter and Marvin Gaye fan, Freddy Cousaert, who whisked him away to Ostend. Cousaert's family welcomed Marvin, and the hospitality so revitalized him that he did several concerts and agreed to a television documentary, called *Marvin Gaye – Transit*

Ostend, which included a memorable unaccompanied version of The Lord's Prayer. Marvin took advantage of the opportunity to clean out his system and Cousaert organised a June tour, despite a tangle of prior agreements and contracts. Marvin had a fruitless meeting with Janis, who returned to America with Bubby, but managed to get through the tour without incident.

The animosity between Marvin and Motown over *In Our Lifetime* was a lasting one, and in April Marvin left the company after 20 years. It was not until nearly a year later that he signed a deal with CBS Records. Berry Gordy surprised Marvin by releasing him from his contract, and the new deal included arrangements for tidying up his financial problems. It had been difficult for CBS vice president, Larkin Arnold to persuade his

Red satin!

company that Marvin might have some steam left in him, and Marvin was determined to justify Arnold's faith in him, even to the extent of giving him artistic control over the new album.

He was working slowly on the new material in June 1982 when he was reunited with Harvey Fuqua. Marvin invited him to Belgium and Fuqua's wisdom and patience brought order to Marvin's tortuous recording process. The catalyst for the songs was some work on lyrics with writer David Ritz, who came up with the phrase 'Sexual Healing'. When the tapes were delivered to CBS in September, the material exceeded even Larkin Arnold's expectations. 'Sexual Healing' was the strongest song and the first single from *Midnight Love*, both released in November 1982. The single reached number 3 in

America and number 4 in Britain, kept off the top by Paul McCartney and Michael Jackson's 'The Girl Is Mine' and Eddy Grant's 'I Don't Want To Dance', respectively. The album got to number 7 in America, selling over two million copies, and to number 10 in Britain.

Because of his financial clean slate, Marvin was able to return to America to help promote the album. He was on good form, able to talk positively about his Motown years and his good fortune with CBS, and a party given in his honour by his new company lasted for two days. And in 1983 he finally turned his previous eight Grammy award nominations into two wins, for Best Instrumental Performance and Best Male Vocal. It was a belated but well-deserved acknowledgement for an artist whose public and contemporaries had held him in

Grammy award, 1983

high esteem for over two decades, with 26 albums and 40 hits.

Marvin made several live and television appearances, including singing the national anthem at the National Basketball Association All Star game, and appearing as one of the highlights of Motown's 25th anniversary show.

It was his family life that created the tragedy of the last few months of Marvin's life. He returned to America, partly because his mother was undergoing a kidney operation; his father had moved back to Washington, so he could be with her during her recuperation. However, the combination of Marvin's return to heavy cocaine use with the return of his father was to prove a deadly one.

Marvin was already in need of money again,

and submitted to an American tour from April to August 1983. His drug intake always increased on the road, but now he was eating and smoking cocaine as well as snorting it. His mental stability quickly deteriorated; it was as though his mind was finally starting to crumble after years of abuse. He became more and more paranoid, believing that someone was out to kill him, and he and his aides began to carry guns. He was hospitalized for a week half-way through the tour.

In August, he retreated to his parents' house and Alberta Gay found herself trapped between Marvin stoned, and her husband, drunk. Although Marvin had several interesting musical projects to work on, he let everything go – he looked terrible, rarely got dressed and there were reports of violence against several women.

Marvin Gaye

His state remained unchanged into the spring of 1984. He would sometimes sit out at the front of the house waving at the cars, and spent a lot of the time watching television and videos. It was on 1 April that the Gay family turned simmering resentment into violence for the last time. It began in the smallest way, with Marvin's father unable to find an insurance document. He went upstairs to where Alberta was talking to Marvin and began to rant at her. Finally roused, Marvin hit his father and pushed him out onto the landing. Marvin Snr went to his room, returned with a .38 revolver which Marvin had given him, and shot his son twice at close range before walking out of the house.

When the ambulance arrived there was a half-hour delay before treatment because the paramedics would not enter the house until the gun had been recovered. It is possible that earlier treatment could have stopped the massive blood loss that killed Marvin Gaye. It was the day before his 45th birthday.

Three days later, ten thousand people filed past the open coffin for a last glimpse of a legend, and two days later his ashes were scattered at sea.